Letters from a Revolution

Letters From a Revolution 1775-1783

A Selection
From the Bronck Family Papers
At the Greene County Historical Society

Edited by RAYMOND BEECHER

Foreword by JOHN H. G. PELL

Published jointly by

The Greene County
Historical Society
Coxsackie, New York

and

The New York State
American Revolution
Bicentennial Commission

Albany, 1973

Foreword

It has been a busy 200 years for the people of New York
State since the Revolution began. To evoke for today's
readers a sense of lives ended so long ago is not easy. But the
distance in time seems less when the distance in space is
reduced — when the knowledge that "they were here"
encourages us to imagine that we were there.

If we had been there, few of us would have been in
uniform and battle. Most of the population then as now must
remain at home, experiencing the fears and deprivations of
war from a distance. It is the special virtue of the documents
Mr. Beecher has edited here that they reflect this kind of
experience in a realistic way. The enterprise he and the
Greene County Historical Society have shown in undertaking
this project is a service to their community and an example
to others.

One of the purposes of the New York State American
Revolution Bicentennial Commission is to encourage just
such thoughtful efforts to commemorate the occasion local-
ly, and it is a special pleasure to lend the Commission's
support to the publication of *Letters From a Revolution.*

John H. G. Pell, *Chairman*
New York State
American Revolution
Bicentennial Commission

1. *Leonard Bronk as seen in the postwar years by the Albany painter Ezra Ames. The portrait is in the Bronx House; photograph by Harry Case, Coxsackie, N.Y.*

Introduction

To mention the wars in American history is to conjure up images of pitched battles between uniformed men glimpsed through clouds of white smoke and flashes of orange fire. The American Revolution is a case in point. The confrontation of Minute Men and British at Lexington Green and Concord Bridge, Washington crossing the Delaware to attack Trenton, the Battle of Yorktown — these are the images we first see in our mind's eye. When one reduces the Revolution to New York State, the process repeats itself. The dramatic capture of Fort Ticonderoga, the Battles of Long Island, Saratoga, Oriskany and Stony Point, the Clinton-Sullivan campaign — these are the highlights of our first reactions.

Rarely do we view the Revolution in the context of the daily existence of a quiet community where no monumental military deeds took place, where men and women suffered without bleeding and fought without seeing their enemy, where the war was first a series of civilian sacrifices and only occasionally a letter or visit from the man who fought the battles recounted in the histories.

The Coxsackie-Catskill area of New York State was such a community during the Revolution. No significant military actions took place there, but its role in the Revolution was nonetheless important. The citizens of this strategically located area made distinctive contributions to the American cause through the more than six years the military conflict was sustained. There is no glamor in producing foodstuffs, draft animals, and fire wood, but without heat, pack trains and rations the American army would have suffered even more than it did. And these were the services to the American cause most of the population was called upon to give, not only in this one small area but elsewhere. The life described in the papers published here was disjointed by Revolution in ways that were seldom dramatic but usually representative.

The central figures in the story that follows are Leonard Bronk, his father, John L. Bronck, and his cousin Leonard

John   Vanette   Casper

Wessell Salisbury   John

Casper v Hellenbergh

John

     Benjamin

     Van den berk

Rudolph Johnson   John

John Voss

Richard   Vandenbergh

Henry Wabber

Witbeck

William Wells

2. *A slightly enlarged section of the columns of signatures to the Coxsackie Association document printed on pages 11–13. The original is in the Albany Institute of History and Art.*

Gansevoort, Jr. Their public and personal documents, with the exception of the first, are part of a large collection of Bronck manuscripts dating from the early colonial period into the mid 1900's.

The Broncks, like many Dutch families, had deep roots in the colony of New York. Their founding father was Jonas Bronck, who settled Bronck's land (the present New York City Borough of the Bronx) in 1639. After his death, the young son Pieter was brought up river when Arent Van Corlear married the widow. As the head of a family, Pieter earned his livelihood in the operation of an Albany tavern. Disputes with local officials concerning unlawful contacts with the Indians as well as difficulties with tavern customers, led Pieter to settle on a patent of land at Coxsackie in 1663. In the next generation, his son Jan held extensive tracts of land both at Coxsackie and at Old Catskill (Leeds). Jan served as a lieutenant with Schuyler's 1705 expedition to Canada.

In subsequent generations the Broncks became prosperous farmers, mill owners, local public officials, militia officers, and small scale land speculators. Transfer of loyalty from the Dutch to the English crown, and then to the revolutionary government, was relatively easy for the Whigs. At the opening of the revolution John Leendertse Bronck (1723–1794), because of wealth, education, and marriage ties with the Gansevoorts, DeWandelaers, Van Burens, Connynes, and other upriver Dutch families, was a person of considerable importance in lower Albany county. Both John L. and his son Leonard (1751–1828) were active supporters of the revolutionary committees and were signers of the declaration of the Coxsackie Association in May of 1775.

This association, following the format ordered by the central committees, became the quasi-legal government for the Coxsackie district. It included the geographical area from present-day New Baltimore on the north, both Coxsackie and West Coxsackie, Athens (Lonenburgh), Leeds (Old Catskill), and open lands to the west. Catskill Landing, which was later to become the present village of Catskill, was not thickly settled until the close of the Revolution and the migration from New England. The Great Imboght was a smaller second association closely allied with Coxsackie. It included the fertile farm region from the wide Hudson

River bay below Catskill inland to the west at the foot of the mountains.

The two districts frequently cooperated in sending elected representatives to the meetings of the central committee at Albany, among whom were John L., Reitsent, Philip, and John Bronck. Throughout the war years these two political groups supported the local militia, controlled the tory population, held elections, allocated salt to well-affected families, met the demands for men and military supplies, and otherwise maintained the fabric of local government. The Great Imboght district occasionally asserted its independence of Coxsackie as is indicated in the dispute over the election of militia officers. An appeal being made to the Committee at Albany, that group urged a geographical compromise. The field officers then elected included Anthony Van Bergen and John L. Bronck as colonel and as second major from Coxsackie; the Great Imboght supplied Cornelius DuBois, Ignas Van Orden, and John Ten Broeck as lieutenant colonel, first major, and adjutant respectively. Lonenburgh was awarded the position of quartermaster which went to Harbartis Van Loon.[1]

As the war progressed more security measures were enforced. Passes were required for civilian travel, tories were apprehended and sent to the Albany jail and eventually to the Fleet prison. Patriots manned the fire signal beacon at the Kykuit and certainly must have seen other such signal fires ablaze at the invasion of the river valley by the British fleet. The firing of Kingston and the burning of the Livingston estate at Clermont raised great apprehension. Stories are still related of the movement of cattle, household and farm equipment to the woods inland from the danger area. The retreat of Sir Henry Clinton's fleet down river after the defeat of General Burgoyne's army at Saratoga for the moment eliminated that danger. Plans to block the channel of the Hudson by sinking sloops near Coeymans were suspended.

The Coxsackie and the Great Imboght districts provided both men and supplies for the revolutionary effort. Unlike the farms in Westchester, the Mohawk Valley, and the Champlain area, theirs were virtually untouched by the conflict. Among the Bronck revolutionary era manuscripts are many indicating the extent to which purchases and impressments of supplies were made on the inhabitants.

Wooden casks, most essential for pork, beef, flour, and other military needs, were in great demand. Staves for their manufacture as well as cord wood for the Albany military barracks required the committees to provide horses, wagons, and drivers to move them.

Leonard Bronk (first to use the simplified spelling of the family name) in 1780 was appointed assistant state agent under Colonel Udny Hay. Bronk's responsibility on a local level lay in coordinating the purchase and impressments of forage, grains, flour, beef, horses, wagons and tackling (harnesses), and shoes and stockings with payment being made in certificates as well as the "new issued" paper currency. The certificates were acceptable for the payment of taxes. Both John L. and his son Leonard also supervised the operation of the family mill to meet the urgent demands for flour. On the lawn at Bronck House Museum are large mill stones which family history indicates were used in the mill to grind grain for the revolutionary troops.

Tories continued to create security problems for the committees. In addition to the tory nest at Kinderhook across the river, loyalists and their sympathizers on the west side of lower Albany county became bolder as the war for independence dragged on. As late as 1778 a party from the neighborhood of Catskill enlisted for the King's service.[2] Urgent pleas were sent to the Albany Committee to reinforce the local militia in patrol duties on the western boundries. Little assistance was forthcoming from the settlers of the interior region. Many had gradually abandoned their farms as the danger from tories and Indians increased. Ulster county became a haven for the patriot families of DeWittsburg (Oak Hill) after the massacre of the Strope family at Round Top.[3] Finding the Greenville land unsafe, Jacob Bogardus returned to Coxsackie for the duration of the war.[4] An Indian-tory raid on the Abeel farm (Catskill-Palenville road) in which David Abeel, among others, was taken prisoner to Canada, indicates the seriousness to which the outlying farms were exposed.[5] The great plain at Patmaskasick (South Cairo — Sandy Plains) was established as a fortified point for scout duties.

Men served the revolutionary cause from both the Coxsackie and the Great Imboght districts. Some enlisted in the line regiments and saw active service in the Continental army, (e.g. Andrew Dunlap and Tunis Van Waganen); others were enrolled in the levies for extended military duty, e.g. Samuel Van Vechten and Philip Conine, Jr.). A third group comprising the local militia was under the command of Colonel Anthony Van Bergen. Both John L. Bronck and his son Leonard were officers in the latter.

The letters written by Leonard Gansevoort, Jr., cousin of General Peter Gansevoort, to Leonard Bronk at Coxsackie reflect some of the revolutionary activities in the City of Albany. Leonard Gansevoort, Jr., had studied law under Peter Van Schaack of Kinderhook, and while practicing law in Albany became very active in support of the new government. He also served as secretary to the County Committee for the Detection and Defeating of Conspiracies.[6] The Gansevoorts and Broncks had long been related since the first Harmen Gansevoort married Maritje Leedertse Conyn about 1670; Jan Bronck had married her sister Commertje. In a subsequent generation Leonard Bronk and Leonard Gansevoort, Jr., had grandmothers who were sisters — namely, Anna and Catarine de Wandelaer. Leedert Bronck and his wife Anna frequently wintered in Albany, strengthening ties with other Dutch families in that city.

The Bronck Revolutionary War manuscripts, as well as those from the Ely family of Connecticut which are not included in this publication, were preserved for the people of this state through the foresight of Leonard Bronk Lampman. They came to the Greene County Historical Society in 1939 as part of a large legacy of real and personal property as a memorial to his mother Adelaide Ely Bronk Lampman. The papers are to be found in the Greene County Historical Society's research library and are available to persons undertaking historical research. The prerevolutionary Bronck Homestead at Coxsackie is the headquarters of the Society.

In editing the surviving papers in this collection, every document selected has been printed in its entirety, and the few omissions have been limited to routine notes which appear never to have been of more than passing interest. The spelling, punctuation and capitalization of the originals has been left untouched in the printing except for some expansion of abbreviations. Where the original could lead to confusion or words needed for coherence are omitted, editorial insertions are supplied in brackets. Spelling and capitalization have been modernized in the notes and index.

Modernization of the style of the texts could have been adopted as a method with good precedent. It would speed up the reading, and it would make the writers seem "closer" to the twentieth century. But the barrier to understanding the original texts is hardly a real problem, and it seems worthwhile to remind today's reader of one way in which the eighteenth century was not close to our own. There was no standard dictionary then, no settled rules for capitalizing and punctuating, and not a great deal of concern about such matters, even among educated men. Thomas Jefferson, writing at the same time as the Broncks and their friends, habitually started his sentences without capitals, and persistently misspelled the names of even close friends.

1. Greene County Historical Society, *The "Old Times" Corner, First Series;* edited by George H. Chadwick and Jessie Van Vechten Vedder (Catskill, N. Y., 1932), p. 31.

2. William L. Stone, *Life of Joseph Brant — Thayendanegea, Including the Indians Wars of the American Revolution,* Vol. 1 (New York, N. Y.: George Dearborn & Co., 1838), p. 356.

3. Jessie Van Vechten Vedder, *History of Greene County 1651 — 1800* (Catskill, N. Y., 1927), p. 77.

4. Vedder, ibid., p. 89.

5. Vedder, ibid., p. 63

6. Alice P. Kenny, *The Gansevoorts of Albany* (Syracuse, N. Y.: Syracuse University Press, 1969), p. 26.

Acknowledgements

Encouragement and technical assistance for this project came from several sources. The New York State Council on the Arts initially supplied a grant-in-aid to catalogue and otherwise put the Bronck manuscripts in condition for serious research. Dr. Louis L. Tucker, State Historian and Executive Director of the New York State American Revolution Bicentennial Commission, conferred with me at the Bronck Museum library in 1972 and felt a printing of selected Bronck manuscripts would be a scholarly contribution to the bicentennial. Dr. Thomas E. Felt, Principal Historian, supplied invaluable technical assistance in the final stages of editing, designed the book, and arranged for its printing. The Director of the Albany Institute of History and Art, Mr. Norman Rice, graciously gave permission for the inclusion of the Coxsackie Association document in their collection, to which Greene County Historian Mabel P. Smith wrote the introductory remarks.

And finally I include my wife Catharine Beecher, who never disturbed the clutter of papers and books in the study, who gave of her time and patience in reviewing notes, proofreading, and otherwise assisted in maintaining a reasonable level of scholarly quality for this publication.

Letters From a Revolution

1   The Association: Coxsackie, May 17, 1775; introductory remarks by Mabel P. Smith, Historian, Greene County Historical Society. In brackets following each name the editor has indicated by a question mark uncertainties in interpreting the spelling of some names, and has expanded other names in accordance with information obtained from other sources, including militia rolls, tax assessment records, and church registers.

Under date of May 17, 1775, more than 220 "Freeholders and Inhabitants of the Cocksakie District in the County of Albany" put their names or marks to a document known to them as "The Association," popularly called "The Coxsackie Declaration" since its discovery in unexplained storage in an Albany attic in 1923. The signed parchment was deposited at Albany Institute of History and Art at that time. A framed photostatic copy is owned by Greene County Historical Society. Bronck House, traditionally identified as a secret meeting place of the local Committee of Correspondence, probably was the temporary repository, in the spring of 1775, of the Association and the place where men of Catskill and the Great Imboght, as well as of Coxsackie, were called to sign. Signatures were evidence of alignment in the controversy with the parent government and authorization of representatives in Provincial Convention and Continental Congress.

The text of the 1775 Association is almost identical with that of the "General Association adopted by the Freemen, Freeholders, and Inhabitants of the City and County of New York, on Saturday, the 29th of April, 1775, and transmitted for signing to all the counties in the Province." (Force's American Archives, 4th ser., v. 3, p. 582.) The signed articles were returnable to the General Committee of New York by July 15. While the text was recorded and published elsewhere in the State, the Coxsackie document seems to be the only original of its kind now surviving, an early product of the awakening spirit of unity and the recognition of a common cause among scattered communities and previously unrelated colonies.

PERSUADED that the Salvation of the Rights and Liberties of America, depends, under God, on the firm Union of its Inhabitants, in a vigorous prosecution of the Measures necessary for its Safety, and convinced of the necessity of preventing the Anarchy and Confusion which attend a Dissolution of the Powers of Government: We the Freeholders and Inhabitants of the Cocksakie District in the County of Albany, being greatly alarmed at the avowed Design of the Ministry to raise a Revenue in America, and shocked by the bloody Scene acting in the Massachusetts Bay; DO in the most solemn Manner, resolve never to become Slaves; and do associate under all The Ties of Religion, Honour, and Love to our Country, to adopt and endeavor To carry into Execution, whatever Measures may be rendered by the Continental Congress, or resolved upon by our Provincial Convention for the purpose of preserving our Constitution, and opposing the Execution of several arbitrary and oppressive Acts of the British parliament, untill a Reconciliation between Great Britian and America, on constitutional principles, (which we most ardently desire) can be obtained; and that we will, in all Things, follow the advice of our general Committee, respecting the purposes aforesaid, the preservation of peace and good Order, and the safety of Individuals and private property. Dated at Cocksakie the Seventeenth Day of May in the year of our Lord One Thousand seven hundred and seventy five

John Schuneman V. D. M.
 [Minister of the Word of God?]
Thennijs Van Vechten [Teunis]
Jas. Barker [James]
Henry Van Bergen
John L Bronck
Jacob Hallenbeck [by mark]
William Halenbeek [by mark]
Anthony Van Bergen
John A Witbeeck [Witbeck]
Saml Van Vechten [Samuel]
Pieter Connyne [Connine]
Thomas Hoghteling
Micheal Collyer [by mark] [Collier]
Francis Salisbury Jr

John Goes [by mark]
Cornelius Connine
Reitsent Bronck
John Hallenbeck [by mark]
John Munday [by mark]
James Donnly [?]
Joseph Groom
Albert Van Loon
Joachim Tryal [Tyron?]
David Rose
Gerardus Neukerk [Newkerk]
Matthias Hallenbeck [by mark]
Storm Rosa
Christian Blodan [?]
John Person

Johannes Jansen [by mark]
Lambert Van Valkenburgh [by mark]
Casper Hellenbeek
Myndert V. Schaick [Van Schaick]
Arent Van Schaick [by mark]
Jacob Van Loon
Jacob Hallenbeck
William Van Bergen
Casper M. Halenbeck
Peter Bronck
Leonard Bronk
Abraham Hallenbeck
Peter Vanette [by mark]
Wilhelmus Vandenbergh
John Vanette [by mark]
Wessell Salisbury
Casper W. Hallenbeck
John G. Voogt
Abraham Salisbury junr.
Reyckert Van den berk
    [Vandenbergh]
Rulik Johnson
John Vosburgh
Richard Vandenbergh [by mark]
Henry Wabber [Webber]
Isaak Witbeck
William Wells
Ban: Staates Salisbury [Barent]
A Damkelten [?]
Ebenezer Stanton
Willm Brandow Junr [William]
Edward Groom
Haederick Schram [by mark]
Clement Overbagh
Benjamine Van gerdener
Frederick Schram
Wm Jones [William]
Reuben Stanton
Andrew Van den berk [Vandenbergh]
Benjamen Sammon
Jno Moore [Johnson]
Isaak Vosburgh [?]
Barent Ebbertson [Egbertson]
Peter Tryon
Benjamin Cornelius Dubois
Benjamin Dubois
Henry Souser
Nikolaes Pare [Parry]
Matthis Van lon Jun [Van Loon]
Casper Pare [Perry]
John Romear
Benjamin Essex [by mark]
John van Stienberg
Gared Peresen [Garrit Persen]
Petrus Souser
John C Claws [Clough, Clow]
Jeremiah Steenbergh [by mark]
John Wall [by mark]

James White [by mark]
John Sinder [by mark]
Nicholas Van Loon
Martin Hallenbeek
[possible signature, illegible]
John V Schaak [Van Schaack]
John V Buche [?]
Nicholas V Schake [Van Schaak]
Peter Van Burgan [Bergen?]
John Parree [Parry]
Isaac Collyer [by mark] [Collier]
Jacob Livingston [?]
Thomas Templer [by mark]
Joseph Nisbit
William Groom
Henry Knoll
John Schrader [by mark]
Arent Goose [by mark]
Hendrick Smith [by mark]
William Smith [by mark]
Geurt Rosa [Gerrit]
Marten G V Bergen [Van Bergen]
Wilhelmius Dedrick [by mark]
Jury Van Loon [by mark]
John Nesderick [?]
Solomon Schut
Nicholaes V Scak [Van Schaak]
Direk Van Veghten [Vechten]
John Vosburgh [?]
Frederick Dederick
Johannie Spoor
Wilhelmus Overbagh [by mark]
Laurence Dubois
John Van Housen [by mark]
William Klauw [by mark] [Clough,
    Clow]
Jome Spoor [?]
Johannie Souser
Petrus Van Loon
Albartus Van Loon
John Rouse
Pet Schram [by mark] [Peter]
Dick Spoor
Andries Eaghlar [by mark]
William Cudney
Fredereck Schut
John Bronck
John Van Loon
Casperse Hallenbeck
Mathias Boom
Peter Janson [?]
Johs. H Schermerhorn [?]
Hugh Deniston
Laurence Winney
Stephen Haight
Cornelius Spoor
Thos Garnett [Thomas?]
John Ellis [?]

John Lampman [by mark]
Mod Van Sand [Van Zandt?]
Heny. Oothoudt [Henry]
Saml Allen [Samuel]
Abraham Camer
Wilhelmus Lampman
Herman Becker [by mark]
Casper Hallenbeek
Nicholas Van Loon
Robert Thomas
Jacob Shoup [Sharp?]
Peter Van Loon Junr
Abraham Van Loon
Hendrick Rose [by mark]
William Rea
Philip Connyne [Connine]
Reyckert Van den berck
    [Vandenbergh]
[?] vaen den Berck [Vandenbergh]
Coenraet Hoghtaline [by mark]
Richard Houghtaline [by mark]
Philip Conine Junr
Baltus Van Slyk [Van Slyck]
John Van den berck [Vandenbergh]
Jeremiah Conine [by mark]
Peter Conine
Peter Van Slyk [Van Slyck]
Jam. Hearn [James]
Abraham Ceater [?]
Peter Chaddere
Philip Bronck
Beniamen Smith
Martin V. Bargan [Van Bergen]
Peter Smith
Petrus Brandow
John Curby
Jacob Van Vechten
Francis Salisbury
Cornelius Dubois
Huybartus Dubois
John Dubois
Benjamin Dubois
Theuny D Van Veghten [Van
    Vechten]
Benjamin Freligh [by mark]
William Brandow [by mark]
Cornelius Schermerhorn
Lyck Van Vleit [?]
Gysbert Oosterhoudt
Jacob Egbersten Junior
Garet Steenbergh [by mark]
Thomas Fish
Egbert Bogardus
Peter Bogardus
Thomas Van Garde [?]
Tomas Aston by order
Jhn Persen [?]

Jonnues Brandow [by mark] [?]
Johannis Conyn [Conine]
John Casperse Van Hoesen
Nicholas Lantman [by mark]
Andries Chnythouse [by mark] [?]
John Dryver [by mark]
Joseph Horsford
Johannes Planke [by mark]
Tomas Burdick by order
Abraham Van Garde by der or [?]
Arent Fedden [by mark]
Taeb Van Waganen by order [?]
Pter Souser by order
Richard Conway
William Schutt [by mark]
John Tayler
Evevret duo [illegible]
Jacob Cooke [by mark]
Goefrie Brandow by order
Conradt Flaake by order

2   *Leonard Bronk to Joseph Forbes; copy of letter.*

Coxseghkie May 19th 1776

DS.

This Comes to Inform you that Last night about 8 O Clock we Recd. a Lettr. by the post Directed to Ms. Polly & Rachael which we Supposed was from you But they Left our house Last Thursday Morning and dont Doubt but what they had a Short passage and hope a pleasant one. I have Nothg. Materiel to Insert as that our Roads are Lind. with Waggons all a going up to Albany to ride provision for our Army in Canada. So I conclude with my Love to you & your family parti: to Mc. R. & CL and do heartily Wish that

       Our king who Reigns below & Above
       Shall Restore to you his Mennifold Love
       and keep you free from Danger
       In haste Dear Sir I Subscribe my Self
       Yr. Most Effectionate friend & Humble Sevt.

Leond. Bronk

3   *Philip Conine, Jr., of Coxsackie; captain in the levies commanded by Lt. Col. Marinus Willett; to Leonard Bronk at Coxsackie.*

Ticonderoga May 28th 1776

Dear Cousin,

Sir I write this Letter to you to hear from you whether you are Dead or not I sent you Now four Letters after Another and Never Received one yet from You I hope you will be kind Enough to send me a Letter Back at the Receiving of this Sir I have to Acquaint you with some Sad News from Canada, I suppose You have heard there was Sent a Regiment to a place calld. the Ceders which we hear from there are Entirely Cut of and taken prisoners Afterward the [they] sent a major to Assist them with a Number of men Not knowing that the Regiment was Cut off and the [they] are also taken and kilt By the Regulars and Indians We further hear that General Arnold is gone up there I suppose you have heard what price General Arnold has took from the Tories what the [they] designed to send to the Regulars there at the Ceders which is as we hear One hundred and twenty six Barrels of Rum, and a great many Other things and some powder and Bawls [balls] which I Cant give an Exact Number of Our army has possession yet of the point shembow which is forty miles on this side of Queback [Quebec] and we are In hopes that we shall keep a stand there which was thought impossible by the most of Gentleman The [they] have made all the fortifications that Ever the [they] could at the River St. Cl. [St. Clair] But we hear that General Thomas is gone Down to the point shambow again with Chief of the army to fortify that place General Sullivan Saild. from here yesterday with his Brigade for Montreal No more as that I am In good health Hoping to hear the same from you and all good Friends to the Cause Be kind Enough to Give my Compliments to your father and mother and all my Loving friends and to all the Ladys at Coxsackie that wishes us well here

    I am Sir your Most Loving Cousin
        Philip Conine
To Mr. Leonard Bronck
NB. our Regiment is partly Stationed at Fort George But our Company is at This place and partly at Crown point When you send me a Letter Direct to Ticonderoga for I suppose we shall stay here yet some time

4   *Samuel Van Vechten of Catskill; captain in Colonel Cornelius D. Wynkoop's Regiment of Militia in the service of the United States of America; to Leonard Bronk at Coxsackie.*

                Skeensborough [Whitehall] 23 Sept 1776
Dear Sir
    Receivd. Yours of the [date left blank] & Shod. have ansrd. it long before but Expectd. another from You soon after agreeable to the Contents of the one You sent as You sead You head no time at that Present time to Enlearge on Acct. of the Great Damage Your Place had sustained by the Uncommon Flood of Water that had been at that Place but would soon after Send another, but have never Receivd. another since You have forgot to Write or wether the Letter is miscarryd. You will best be able to judge I have this Month Past been very much Troubld. with the Fevour Ego [ague] every other Day which hes made me very week &

Poor: it is the unwholesomet. Place that Ever was known in this World Their hes scarcely been a Men on this Ground for Two or Three weeks but what hes head that Disagreeable Distamper or Something worse but thank God I have got the Better of it for I have not head it these 4 Days last past & hope it may not lay hould of me again. I have but little News from the Northd. Only this morning we was informd. that the Same Officer that head Killed B.D. General Gorden at or near St. Johns Some time ago: hes Since that been Sent out again He & another Man & are returnd. at Ticonderoga & have brought in Two Prisoners The one was a Quarter-Master & the other a souldier of the Rigulers Thay whare taken near St. Johns What acct. thay give from the Rigular Army we have not yet been able to learn The News of Ms. Annatie Van Orden being very unexpected to me as I head never heard of the Courtship; however if they make a Happy pair I am glead of the Match As Milligen is an ould Souldier & I think a good Souldier I make no doubt but he will do his Endeavour to make some Young ones which I Can't but Recommend to every one as Souldiers is a great Call for in these Trouble some Times I am with my Best Respects after Beaging the Favour of being Remembered to Your father Mother the Ladies Ms. Polly & Rachael Coxseghkie Ms Tyne & all the Rest of the Coxseghkie & the Catskill Ladies, Your Moust Humble Sarvt.

Sam. Van Vechten

5 *Philip Conine, Jr., of Coxsackie; captain in the levies commanded by Lt. Col. Marinus Willet; to Leonard Bronk at Coxsackie.*

Skensborough [Whitehall] 12th Febry 1777

Loving Friend

I do take the Earliest opportunity to acquaint you that I am Stationed at this place till further orders from the General But I am this minute Arrived from Ticonderoga There are but very few Troops at that place I dont think there is any Danger at that place for the Ice is but very poor in the Lake which will prevent the Enemy from Coming over Ticonderoga is well fortified I dont think if there is Sufficient Number of Troops send there that it will be taken without Providence is against us I should feel very happy to see you here next summer I have Nothing New to Write to you from this post I do Expect you shall send me a Letter by the First Opportunity and what News from the Jerseys I am in good health Hoping to hear the same of you, I am with Respect your Loving friend In haste the man is waiting for the Letter

Philip Conine

NB. Be good Enough when you See any of my fathers family to Acquaint them I am in good health Remember me to all the Ladies

6 *Leonard Gansevoort, Jr., of Albany; to Leonard Bronk at Coxsackie.*

Albany 16th May 1777

Dr Sir

I received your kind Favour of the 14th May by Mr. Peter Elting I shall purchase the Tickets for you immediately and hope you may be as fortunate as you can possibly wish to be The highest Prize however you must not aspire to as I put in for it

I am extreamly sorry to hear that the Tories are the Cause of Disquiet to you They have given us great trouble but I hope they are so well secured at the least the Heads of them that we have not much Danger to apprehend for the future Next Monday the Court Martial constituted for the Trial of the Tories confined in goal meets I hope they make an Example of some villians There are those who richly deserve the Gallows

I inclose you a Letter for Arent Van Schaack your Neighbour which I would be glad if you would deliver him

Respects to your Father and Mother I had almost forgot to tell you that John DeWandelaer is married

Your Friend
L. Gansevoort Junr.

7   *Philip Conine, Jr., of Coxsackie; captain of the levies commanded by Lt. Col. Marinus Willett; to Leonard Bronk at Coxsackie.*

Fort Schuyler 27th June 1777

Dr. Friend
   Sir
   I take this favourable opportunity to Acquaint you that I am in good health Hoping to hear the same from you & all good friends I am Sorry to Acquaint you that two Days ago a Private Soldier was Barbarusly killed by the Indians & a Captain Shot threw the Body & Schulped But is a live as Yet The Doctor says that he may Posible Recover But I look upon the wound to be mortally
   We have nothing more at this Place But should be Extremely Glad to hear from you & some of my good friends We have not had a Single Syllable of News from below this some time Should be glad to hear from the Coxsackie gentlemen and Ladies No more In great Hast am with Respect your friend & Humble servant
                                       Philip Conine

per favour of Mr. Hansen

8   *Philip Conine, Jr., of Coxsackie; captain in the levies commanded by Lt. Col. Marinus Willett; to Leonard Bronk at Coxsackie.*

Fort Schuyler 27th July 1777

Dear Leonard
   I have Recieved yours of the 9th July with the Agreeable News that you being in good health, which Blessing I Now again do Enjoy But have Lately been Very unwell We have Nothing New at this place We have Expected the Enemy would have been here before this time by what accounts we Received from the Indians I am this minute a going Down to Onida Lake on a Scout and on our Return are to stop up the Passage of Wood Creek. Capt. Bleeker Comands our Party which thus Consist of fifty Continental Troops & Sixty malitia I hope No bad News Shall be heard from this Quarter Our men are in high Spirits & dont make any Doubt if the Enemy thus appear but what you shall hear the [they] shall meet with a Drubbing This minute

after beginning to write an alarm happened hear by our working Party who fired on a Scout of Indians but did not kill any The Indians Run of [off] No more am in great heast for the party waits for me

Be good Enough to give my Compliments to all our Ladies & Gentlemen and My kind Love to your father & Mother I am Sir Your Most Humble Sevt.

Philip Conine

NB. I do Expect to come down in about Seven weeks if nothing thus happen hear Extraordinary

9 Andrew Dunlap of Coxsackie; corporal in Captain Samuel Van Vechten's company of militia of Colonel Cornelius D. Wynkoop's battalion in the service of the United States of America; to Leonard Bronk at Coxsackie.

Camp near Still Water Sept. 16th 1777

Dr. Sir

I take this Opportunity to inform you that I am in good health Hoping these few lines may find you and all your fathers Family the same

All the news I have at Present is that ever Since we have Been incamped here we have been Fortifying and this morning have been on the parade since Four OClock and Expect every Minute that we Shall have a General Engagement as the Enemy is advancing towards us. I would be glad to hear of you by Every opportunity Pray, Remember my love to Mr Tryons family

Tunis Van Waganen is in Good health and Desires to be remembered to you and fathers Family and to all Inquiring Friends and Desires of you as Henry Souser has Deserted to Take him Up He had no time [to] Write Should have Wrote more particularly to you

I Remain your loving
and Affectionate friend and humble Servant
Andrew Dunlap

By favour of Jonathan Palmer

10 *Tunis Van Waganen; lieutenant in Colonel Philip Van Cortland's second regiment, the line, in the service of the United States of America; to Leonard Bronk at Coxsackie.*

Camp Valley Forge January 20th 1778

Dear Sir

These are to inform you that I am as yet in a good State of Health Together with all the Lads from your Quarter Hoping these may find you and all good friends the Same

I have not much news at present But that our people have taken a Rich prize from the Enemy on the River Delaware

I should be glad to have a few lines from you by the first opportunity

Conclude with Remaining your
Most Obdt. Humbe. Servant
and Affectionate Friend
Tunis V Waganen

11 *Andrew Dunlap of Coxsackie; corporal in Captain Samuel Van Vechten's company of militia of Colonel Cornelius D. Wynkoop's battalion in the service of the United States of America; to Leonard Bronk at Coxsackie.*

Valley Forge January 24th 1778

Everd. Honourd. Friend

I Look on this Present time As A favourable Opportunity to Wright to One Who I Must and Am Duty Bound to Say Am More A father or Relation By Behaviour than Only Am Friend, But Not Doubting that Your Generous Kind Nature Will Be Rewarded in A Satisfactiros Manner

Being willing to acquaint You that I Am Very Happly in Having my Health At This Present time And Moreso A Stedfast Resolution to Remain a Strong Libertine As Long as My Much Ronged Country May Call for Soldiers Sword and Ball Aspecially Against So Cruel Unjust Barbarious and Abrupt An Enemy, Not Doubting but We Come of [off] Victorious

We Am in the Above Named Place, West from Philadelphia About 21 Miles Where we Have Good Comfortable Hutts Nothing Strange Haith Happined Only on the 19th Ult. Capt. Lee With 1 Sub. 1 Corpl. and 4 Privates was Attacted by a Detacment of 200 of the Dragons They being Housd. Maraceslously Drove the Enemy Leaving 2 Dead and 4 Wounded

Your Humble Servt.
Andrew Dunlap

Desiring So Kind as to favour Me in Remembering My Kind Respects to Rachiel Detherick And Phany Irion And their Respective families and all Enguring friends I Have Hopes of Comeing Home Soon.

12 *Tunis Van Waganen; lieutenant in Colonel Philip Van Cortland's second regiment, the line, in the service of the United States of America; to Leonard Bronk at Coxsackie.*

Head Quarters [Valley Forge]
April 23d. 78 [1778]

Dear Sir

Received your kind favour of the 2 Inst. and am very glad you & relations are well We hear that Col. Van Schaicks Regt. is on their March for this place and that our Regt. is ordered to the Highlands If that is the Case you may expect to see me next Pingster [late spring flowering shrub] [Easter]

Am very glad to hear that you are in so good a posture of Defence in the Highlands

As to news here we have none of Consequence

Am under many Obligations to you for favouring me with a Disposition of the Ladies in your Quarter, am very glad that in your Opinion they are Disposed to favour Gentlemen with their Agreeable Company But I am sure you ought to Condole with me for the Difficulties I undergo that is Absent from them all while you & the rest of your Neighbouring young Gentlemen are Enjoying the Sweets and ease of a private Life Tho I think if I was there this moment I should find out whether they were the Genuine thing or not or I much mistaken

And as to their Longing for Matrimony with those that are agreed I Join you in the Sentiments and are of Opinion that a great many young men are rather Dilatory or they would relieve Some of the Suffering Ladies

I dont say this as a reflection on you It is only an observation on some others of my Acquaintance You may read those two Clauses to Jacob Van Vechten

Am glad to hear that you was with my favorites as you

stile them, am glad you entertain so high an opinion of them I Sympathize with the former as much as yourself for the Loss of her Mother, and you may be Sure that I am happy to think that I am not out of memory tho absent and Shall expect to hear further from Sir

Your Affectionate Friend
& Humbl. Servent
Tunis Van Waganen

13 Andrew Dunlap of Coxsackie; corporal in Captain Samuel Van Vechten's company of militia of Colonel Cornelius D. Wynkoop's battalion in the service of the United States of America; to Leonard Bronk at Coxsackie.

Head Quars. Valley Forge
April 23d 1778

Dear Sir

I embrace this as a favourable Opportunity to inform you that I am safely Arrived at the above mentioned place where I found our Regiment I have seen your Old Acquaintance Mr. Allen Adjutant to Coll. Jacksons Regt. at this place He Desires to be remembered to you

I can with pleasure inform you that I am well Hope these may find you and fathers family the same together with all old Acquaintances

Should be happy If I could send you some news But what we have is To immaterial that it is not worth notice You will Do me a favour to Give my Compliments to Betsy Tryon, Rachel Dedrick & Fanny Tryon and their Respective families

Am Sir your Affectionate Friend
Andrew Dunlap

14 Cornelius D. Wynkoop, commissioner, May 21, 1778 to Leonard Bronk at Coxsackie.

Sir

I Beg of you to Direct the Bearer where he shall find Two of the Continental horses which are in best order & fittest for Service. I know there is some in your neighborhood but I cannot Direct him to the particular house. I am

Sir yours &c
Corn. D. Wynkoop one of
the Com'srs of the State of New York

Coeymans
21th May 1778
P.S. Please to Keep Some more Bran for and hogs Cornell when you get any

15 *Leonard Gansevoort, Jr., of Albany; to Leonard Bronk at Coxsackie.*

Albany 1 Sept 1778

Sir

I expected before now to have heard from you respecting the Flour which I spoke to you about I would be glad if you would let me know whether you have it to spare I am greatly in Want of it as I have not any to use at this Time

We have nothing new at this Time but that two Men have been scalped at Fort Schuyler and three taken Prisoner at Cherry Valley by the Indians

Your Neighbour Jacob Halenbeeck was this Morning brought to Goal I believe it will go hard with him if the Information against him be true

Your Friend
L. Gansevoort Junr.

16 *Warrant from justices of the Coxsackie and the Great Imboght Districts authorizing Constable Philip Vosburgh to impress horses, wagons and drivers to transport cord wood from Coeymans to Albany for the use of the military barracks. Dated Coxsackie September 9, 1778.*

County of Albany
Coxhacky District   To Philip Vosburgh Constable
Whereas Application has been Made to us to Supply a Number of Waggons for the Public Service, to Ride Wood at Coyemans AND Whereas by an Act of the Legislature of this State passed the 2d of Aprill 1778 it is Directed that the Justices or any one of them upon such Application & shall grant a Warrant to Impress Horses and Carriages with Drivers These are to Command in the Name of the People

of the State of New York Immediately and without Delay
to Impress of the Persons Mentioned Opposite to their
Names for the said Service to Proceed to Coyemans to Ride
Cord Wood for the Number of Eight Days unless Sooner
Discharged They are to set out for the said Service on
Friday the Tenth Inst. at 8 Oclock in the morning Those
that are to give Horses to bring them to the place of the
Waggon and Drivers to go there also The Horses to be
furnished Forage by the Owners & the Drivers to furnish
himself for and During the ofd. Service If you find the
Horses and Waggons of such Persons as are Mentioned and
the Drivers to be unable & not Sufficient You are to Impress
such others in there stead as You Shall Judge Can Spare the
same and are Sufficient A Return of Your Proceedings
with this Receipt you are to make to us by the 13th Inst.
hereof Fail not Given under our Hands this 9th Day of
Sept 1778

Heny. Oothoudt	Saml. Van Vechten	John L Bronck
Philip Connyne	Justices	

17 *Warrant from Samuel Van Vechten, justice of the
peace, authorizing Philip Bronck and Edward Groom to
impress several named residents of the Coxsackie district for
twenty tons of hay and 250 bushels of grain to be used by
the army. Dated Coxsackie, April 5, 1779.*

Coxhackie Destrict
Albany County
Whereas by an Act of the Legislature of the State of New
York Passed the Second Day of April in the Year of our
Lord one thousand Seven Hundred & Seventy Eight Entitled
an Act for Regulating of Impresses of Forage & Billitting of
Troops Within this State, it is Enacted that when ever a
Suffetient Quantity of Forage Cannot be purchased Therein
or procured from the Naighbouring States by the Commis-
sary or Deputy Commissary of Forage or by the Forage
Master for the use of the Army in this State that then on
Due Proof thereof on Oath and Application made to any
justice of the Peace resident in the District in which an
Impress is Required it Shall and may be Lawful for the Said
justice and he is hereby Required Immediately Thareupon
by Warrant or Warrants under his Hand to appoint Such &

So many Diferent & prudent Inhabitants of the said State Actually Resident in the Said District & thereby to authorize and Direct him or them to Destrain and take from the Inhabitants of the Said District the Quantity of Forage to be Specified in the Said Warrent And Whareas Mathias Van Lone [Loon] Junr. one of the Deputy Commissioners of Forage of the United States of America on the Day of the Date hereof hath made Oath before me that a suffetient Quantity of Forage Cannot be purchased in this State for the use of the Army in the Same or procured from the Naighbouring States and thareupon made application to me as one of the justices of the Peace Resident in the Destrict of Coxhacky in the County of Albany that an Impress might be made in the Said Destrict of Forage Agreeable to the Directions of the said act in the Quantity of Forty Tons of Hay and Five Hundred Bushels of Barly Rye Oats Indian Corn or Buck Wheat for the use of the Said Army I do therefore in Pursuance of the said Act appoint Edward Groom & Phillip Bronck being Both Inhabitants & Residents of the said District of Coxhacky and I do hereby Authorize & Direct them to destrain and take of and from Isaac Witbecke Lawrence V. Boskerk Jogem Jansen Teunis D Van Vechten Kasper W. Halenbecke Johannes Brandow William Groom Jan Kasperse Van Hosen Nicholas Lampman Kasper Van Hosen Kasper I Halenbacke John M Van Lone Albartes Van Lone Jurry Van Lone Jurray G. Klaw Frederick Lampman Kasper Halenbecke Evert Everse Arent Van Schak Junr. Teunis Van Vechten Inhabitants of the Said Destrict of Coxhacky the Quantity of Twenty Tons of Hay and Two Hundred & fifty Bushels of Barly Rye Oats Indian Corn Buck Wheat being part of the Forage above Specified and Required If their shall be so much Forage over and above what Shall on enquiry by them be found in their openion Necessary for the Subsistance of the respective Families and Stock bone fied keept by Each of the Said Inhabitants And I do hereby Require them in the Execution of this Warrant to Follow the Directions of the a foresaid Act Given under my Hand this 5th Day of April 1779 Saml. Van Vechten justice.

I do hereby Certify that the Within Named Edward Groom and Phillip Bronck on the [date left blank] Day of April one Thousand Seven Hundred & Seventy Nine at the Dwelling House of Lambert Van Valkenburgh Situate at

Coxhackie in the County of Albany have Taken the
Following Oath that they would to the best of their ability
skill and judgment Honestly Deligent Impartially Without
Fear favour Revange or hope of Reward Exacute the Trust
and Duty reposed in an enjoined on them by the within
Warrent Given under My Hand the Date above

Saml. Van Vechten   justice

*18   Thomas Sickels, deputy quartermaster general, to the
justices in the District of Coxsackie; requesting assistance in
the procurement of horses and wagons to move supplies for
the military in the Mohawk Valley.*

Albany June 8th 1779

Gentlemen

   As a Number of Waggons, Horses, and Drivers are
immediately wanted for a Particular Piece of Service I must
request that you will give the Bearer Mr. John I Wendell
every assistance the Law puts in your Power to enable him
to get every waggon & span of Horses in your District   They
must be ordered to Schenectady, after there arrival there,
they will be wanted six or seven Days in Service when they
will be Discharged The General expects that the Mages-
trates in the Different Districts will do every thing in their
Power to procure the waggons & or other wise on this
emergency we will be under the Necessity of sending Troops
for the Purpose

I am Sir
Your Hum Servt
Thos. Sickels
D Q M Genl

*19   Matthew Visscher, corporation clerk for Albany, to the
magistrates, field and other officers and inhabitants of the
District of Coxsackie and the District of the Great Imboght.*

Albany 14th June 1779

Gent.

   The Absolute necessity there is for a Number of Waggons
speedily to Carry on the public Operations to the Westward,
renders it our Indispensible duty as friends and Welwishers
to our Country, to Urge you to an Exartion of your good

offices and Power to get as many Waggons in your District as possible For without waggons are procured the Operations cannot be carried on And we Wish people to Consider that an Immeadiate Exertion in this Matter will not only forward the public business but be the means of securing our Frontiers and Easing the Militia in Military Duty

Should you not be able to get Waggons in an Easy way Let your Militia Officers turn out a party of Men to take and bring them to this place They will only be wanted for Seven or Eight days from their Arrival at Schenectady In full Confidence of your Exertions in this Matter

We Remain your Most
Humble Servts.
By Order of the Corperation
Matt. Visscher Clark [Clerk]

20 *Supervisors of Albany County to the assessors of the District of Coxsackie, authorizing a tax levy of forty five pairs of shoes and eighty five pairs of stockings for the use of the military forces. Dated Albany July 14, 1779.*

By Virtue of an Act of the people of the State of New York entitled "An Act to procure a further supply of Shoes and Stockings for the Troops raised under the direction of this State" passed the 8th Day of March 1779.

You and each of you are hereby directed with all convenient speed, duly and impartially to make a rate of Forty five pair of Shoes and Eighty five pair of Stockings, upon all the Inhabitants of Ward Town Manor District or precinct for which you are chosen assessor or assessors, and to determine the Number of pair of Shoes and Stockings, which the Inhabitants ought respectively to furnish, and who in your Judgment can best spare or procure the Same.

Given under our Hands this 14. July 1779

Isaac Vrooman
Lucas Van Veghten
Stephen Hogeboom
Marcus Bellinger
John L. Bronck
Philip Rockefeller

To
   The Accessors of
   Coxsackie District

Isaac Fonda
John Younglove
Abraham Cuyler
Cornelius Van Veghten

21 *Albartus Van Loon of Lonenburgh [Athens]; character and loyalty recommendation from Whig neighbors and Justices Samuel Van Vechten and Philip Collyer as required by regulation for the licensing of tavern keepers. Such licenses were denied to tory sympathizers; the fee was an important source of revenue. Dated September 19, 1779.*

At the Request of Albartus Van Loon of Lonenburgh [Athens] We the Subscribers do hereby Certify that he is of good and honest fame & Reputation and well Attached to the freedom and Independence of the United States and a man Capable in all Respects for keeping a public house or Tavern   Given under our hands this 19th day of September 1779

Nikolaes Pare
Johannis Cony
Dirk Spoor
Anthony Van Bergen
Myndert Van Schaick
Saml. Van Vechten
Philip Collyer   Justices

22 *Assessment roll prepared by John L. Bronck, Albartus Van Loon, Henry Van Bergen, Friederick Schmid, Martin G. Van Bergen, and Reitsent Bronck on the inhabitants of the Coxsackie District to meet the demand for military supplies of beef as ordered by the legislature meeting at Kingston. Dated at Coxsackie June 21, 1780.*

An Assessment of Twenty five Head of Cattle Assigned by the Legislature of the State for the Quota of the District of Coxsackie And to be delivered from the 25th day of June to the 25th day of October Next   Viz Five Each Month and are as follows

To be delivered on the
25th Instant

To be delivered on the
25 July

Baltus Van Slyck an Ox
Anthy V Bergen A Bull
Teunis V Vechten one
Joseph Groom one
Isaac Colyer one

Arent Van Schaaick a Bull
Marten Hallenbeck an Ox
Jan Van Loon one
Wm Hallenbeck one
Jacob Hallenbeck one

To be delivered on the
25th August
Sartie Hooghtaling an Ox
John L Bronck a Bull
Albert V der Sea an ox
Matth. V Den Berk an Heifer
Jacobus V Slyck one

To be delivered on the
25th of September
Jurry Van Loon A Bull
Caspar Janse Hallenbeck one
Joachim Jansen An Ox
Lambt. V. Valkenburgh An Ox
Mindert Van Schaaick one

To be delivered on the 25th of October

Henry Van Bergen A Bull
Esther Hoghtaling One
Richard Hooghtaling A Cow

Johannes Diedrick One
Jan Caspar V Husen A Cow

Given under our Hands this 21st day of June 1780

John L Bronck   Henry Van Bergen   Marten G V Bergen
Albartus Van Loon Friederick Schmid   Reitsent Bronck
Assessors of the District of Coxackie

23 *Anthony Van Bergen of Coxsackie, colonel of eleventh regiment, Albany County militia; to Leonard Bronk at Coxsackie.*

Coxseghkie 14th July 1780

Sir

You are hereby Ordered & Commanded to Warn the Men In the Inclosed Class Roll to meet at such place as you shall appoint to furnish me an able bodied men Agreeable to law for to Serve in the Company for the space of Three Months unless sooner Discharged The men must be Ready to March with three Days provision on the 21st Inst; You will likewise make a Return to me on the 20th Inst. of the Men you furnished as I am under the necessity to Make a Return to his Excellency the Governor. They are to March on Tuesd. to the house of Thomas Steinbergh at Satireties [Saugerties] to go from there to the place of rondezvous at Fish kill. And in Case of Failure You will be Dealth with According to Law

Anthony Van Bergen Collo. [Colonel]

24 *Warrant from G. V. Schaick [Goose Van Schaick] of Albany authorizing the impressment of flour and meat for the army, August 7, 1780; to Leonard Bronk at Coxsackie.*

By Virtue of the power & Authority to me given by his Excellency George Clinton, Governor of the State of New York, General & Commander in Chief of All the Militia & Admiral of the Navy of the same.

To Leonard Bronck Greeting.

The Occasion & Emergency requiring the same You are hereby Authorized to empress, Ten Tons Flour, or an Equivalent in wheat, & Twenty Thousand weight of Beef, or Fat Cattle Equivalent thereto, For the use & Service of the Army, For doing of which, this shall be Your Warrant.

Given under my hand at Albany this seventh day of August, in the Fifth year of the Independance of the said State, & in the Year of Our Lord, one Thousand, seven hundred & Eighty.

G V Schaick

25 *Leonard Bronk of Coxsackie, assistant state agent; record of accountability for blank certificates used in the procurement of military supplies; to Isaac Stoutenburgh at Albany.*

Coxseghkie 23rd August 1780

Sir

Recd. Augst. 27th 1780 of Isaac Stoutenburgh Esqr. Superintendent for the State Agency in the Counties of Alby. and Tryon 125 Blank Certificates from 798 to 922. both Number Inclusive Recd. Afterwards of R. Lusk 44 Bl. Certif:

Leond. Bronk

Afterwds. 40 Certificates

26 *Assessment roll prepared by Friederick Marden [Marten]; Sybrant Van Schaick, Junior; and Christian Meyer on the inhabitants of the Great Imboght District to meet the demand for military supplies of beef as ordered by the legislature meeting at Kingston. Dated at Coxsackie August 26, 1780.*

An Assessment Roll of the Great Imboght District in the County and pursuant of a Letter of the Legislature of this State, New York Signed by the Hon Pierre Van Cortlandt Lieut Govener & Evert Banker Esq Speaker of the House of an Assembly Dated at Kingston June 12th 1780

Beeves

Abram Person Senr.	1	
Gosah Van Schaick	1	by the 25 September
John Ten Broeke	1	
David Dumond	1	
John B Dumond	1	by the 25th October
Christian Myer	1	by the 25 September
Hezekiah Van Orden Esq	2	

August the 26th, 1780
Friederick Marden
Sybrant V: Schaick Junr.　　　Assessors
Christian Meyer

27 *Benjamin Hicks, captain first New York regiment, to Leonard Bronk at Coxsackie.*

Albany 9th Dec. 1780
This may certify that the bearer Leonard Bronck Esq. has Transported a Waggon Load of Baggage belonging to the first New York Regt. from Hornbeck's to this place being Twenty Nine miles

Benjn. Hicks Capt.

28 *John L. Bronck, supervisor of the Coxsackie District;*
public notice of hearing of loyalty, December 30, 1780.

Copy of the Different Returns of the Capts. Commanding
Companys in Coxseghkie Dist. whose son or sons are Deemed
to have gone of [off] to and joined the Enemy. Agreeable to
a Law of this State passed October 9th 1780

Frederick Cruyslar	1 son	Named	Peter Cruyslar
Jocham Jansen	2 Do.	Do.	Johannis Jansen
			Roudolph Jansen
Widow Cook	1 Do.	Do.	Jacob Cook
Stephen Van Dyck	1 Do.	Do.	Mathies Van Dyck
Jane Dies	2 Do.	Do.	Matthew Dies
			Jacob Dies
John Van Gorden	1 Do.	Do.	Benjn. Van Gorden
Nicholas Pronck	1 Do.	Do.	Nicholas Pronk
William Schram	2 Do.	Do.	Felty Schram
			Frederick Schram
Isaac Colyer	1 Do.	Do.	Dirick Colyer
Henry Knoll	1 Do.	Do.	Michel Knoll
Frederick Lantman	3 Do.	Do.	Peter Lantman
			Frederick Lantman
			Helmus Lantman
Martin Halenbeck	1 Do.	Do.	Jasper Halenbeck
Phillip Connine	1 Do.	Do.	Leonard Connine
Samuel Van Pelt	1 Do.	Do.	Samuel Van Pelt

These are to Notify the above-mentioned persons that the
Supervisor and Assessors of Coxseghkie District will be
Convened on Saturday being the 2th of January Next at the
house of Isaac Witbecks in said District in Order to hear the
Proofs and Alligations of such persons who do appear to
shew Cause why they should not be Assessed Agreeable as
the Law Directs. Given under my [hand and seal] Coxseghkie Dec. 30th 1780

John L. Bronck Supervisor

29 *John L. Bronck of Coxsackie; Soldiers' Song; either composed or copied by him in 1780.*

How stands the Glass around
Of which we take no care my Boys
How &c &c &c
Let mirth & Wine abound
Let the trumpet sound
And Cannons they do roar my Boys
To hurt kill & wound
May we still be found
Content with our hard fate my Boys
On the cold ground.
O! Why Soldiers why
O! Why so melancholy Boys
O! Why &c &c &c
Whose business is to die
Sigh fie & cry
Damn fear drink on my jolly Boys
To him you or I
Through cold wet and dry
We are always bound to follow Boys
We scorn to fly.
It is but in vain
I mean not to upbraid you Boys
It is &c &c &c
For Soldiers to complain
For the next Campaign
Sends us to him that made us Boys
Free from all pain
But should we remain
A Bottle and a kind landlady
Cures all again.

30 *Wilhelm Ryckman, ensign, first New York regiment, February 2, 1781, to John L Bronck at Coxsackie.*

This Certifies that John L Bronk has Boarded and found five Men & one Officer in provision & Lodging Three Days and one Span of horses in Forage They being on Command Coxseghkie Feb. 2nd 1781

Wilke. Ryckman Ensn. [Ensign]
first New York regiment

31 Philip Conine, Jr., of Coxsackie, captain in the levies commanded by Lt. Col. Marinus Willett; to Leonard Bronk at Coxsackie.

Patmaskasick 24 May 1781
[South Cairo Great Plain]

Sir

I Received yours of the 21st Instant The Letter and Commissions you mention are Safe come to hand In my Letter from Colonel Willett he informs me that he will see me Imediately furnished with Ammunition Camp Kettles & paper If there Should be any of those Articles for me at or about Coxsackie I should be most Oblidge to you if you would see it forwarded to me as soon as Possible ·

I am Sorry to Inform you that the Inhabitants of this District are so neglectful in Sending Provision for there men, in particular from Lansingburgh and the flatts, & also some of my neighbours at this place Some Classes have had there men out of Provision for two Days And when I send a man they will only give him two or three Days provision at a time, at which rate it takes my men half that time to go after provisions Lieut. Van Bergen is this morning gone to Livingstons manor in order to receive some men at that place, how they will be furnished With provision I do not yet know I Every minute Expect Lieut. Van Valkenburgh in from a Scout that has been to Schoharry Kill and Batawvia or at Least the time they should return is to Day I have Constant Scouts out but have not made no Discoveries as yet I do remain your Effectionate friend and Humble Servt.

Ph. Conine

32 Philip Conine, Jr., of Coxsackie, captain in the levies commanded by Lt. Col. Marinus Willett; to Leonard Bronk at Coxsackie.

Patmiskasick 26th May 1781
[South Cairo Great Plain]

Sir

I have Received two men from Colonel Rensselaers Regt. of malitia and Expect in a few Days to have a full Company at this place How and in what manner they Will be Supplied with provisions I do not know If you have any publick

Provisions on hand, or could get any I wish it might be forwarded to me, and will give Receipt for the same

I have wrote a Letter to Colonel Van Bergen on the subject. Supposing the District might fall upon Some plan to Victual the troops, I could wish the Inhabitants to Exert themselves on this occasion, or will be oblidge to impress from the Inhabitants, which I should be Exceedingly Sorry for

> I am Sir with Sinceer
> Respect your Humble Servt.
> Ph. Conine Capt.

To Leonard Bronck
Agent to Coxsackie District

I think if an officer was to go Round by the Inhabitants there might be provision Collected, but as my officers are busy to Collect the troops, I wish some of the Officers of malitia would undertake this

33 *Leonard Gansevoort, Jr., of Albany; to Leonard Bronk at Coxsackie.*

Albany 15 August 1781

Dear Sir

I had intended to write you a Letter by your Man Francis but his Departure was so sudden as not to admit of my writing by him

As the Winter Season is approaching it becomes me like the Ants while it is Time to provide for a Supply for that barren Season, Polly says she wants Butter and reckoning you among the Number of her best Friends she has requested me to apply to you to procure it for her Your Mother is in my opinion the only Person who is likely to supply her Wants and she therefore begs you will apply to her for it I have a Butter Keg at Hanse Spoors which I would be glad you would when it is convenient send for and have it filled Polly also begs you would speak to your Mother for a Couple Pounds of Wool

Francis has been very unfortunate while on his Travels I suppose he has by this Time related to you his different adventures The whole City came to see him when he was last Sunday brought in under Guard

General Starks is in Town I have waited on him He talks

as if he will have no occasion for the Militia of this County
this Campaign, a Circumstance which I believe neither of us
will repine at

To the Southward all is quiet   They seem to have come to
a very good Understanding betwixt them, but this is not a
Month to fight   Next Month I believe Matters will begin
to look serious

To the North & westward all is Peace and I hope it may
remain so

Tell your Mother by no Means to let her Spirits fail her, all
will and must in the End be well

My Respects to your Father   Polly joins me in wishing
you and Tyney Health and Happiness

> Your Friend &c.
> L. Gansevoort Junr.

34 *Commissioners for Conspiracies to Leonard Bronk at
Coxsackie. Thomas Gay proved not to be as dangerous as
suggested below. See Leonard Gansevoort, Jr.'s letters of
November 4, 1781 and December 1781. Leonard Bronk also
spoke on his behalf.*

Albany 19 Sept 1781.

Sir

We have received Information that Thomas Gay who
resides near you is a very dangerous Person and have thought
proper in Consequence thereof to send the Bearer Philip
Herwig with a Party of Men to apprehend him   We could
wish you to direct Herwig where to find Gay   We are
induced to believe that Gay is possessed of Papers which
would be of infinite Service to us and would be glad if you
would assist Herwig in searching for such Papers and if any
you find to seal them up & transmit them to us by Herwig

> We are
> Your humb. Servants
> Sam. Stringer   Commissrs.
> John M. Beeckman   for
> Isaac D. Fonda   Conspiracies

*35 Leonard Gansevoort, Jr., of Albany; to Leonard Bronk
at Coxsackie.*

Albany 25th Sept. 1781

Dear Sir

Yours was delivered me by Mr. Gay Appearances are against him and the Commissioners certainly had good Cause for their Conduct towards him I can assure you I never was more surprized in my Life than when I heard him accused It was some Time before I could believe it, and even then not till his Person and Place of Residence were described beyond the Possibility of a Doubt Your Letter to me in his Favour has procured him the Indulgence which he doubtless will mention to you

I thank you for the care you have taken of my Keg.

We have no news from the Southward We are all anxious to hear the Event of the Operations in that Quarter As soon as we receive any Intelligence that may be depended upon I shall let you know

I am in great Haste or I would write you a great Deal and particularly about Mr. Gay When you come up you shall hear the whole I still look upon Gay to be an honest Fellow which I have always taken him for

Your's in Great Haste

L G Junr.

*36 Stephen Haight, merchant of Lonenburgh [Athens],
September 26, 1781; to Leonard Bronk at Coxsackie. The
report below that Cornwallis "was taken" was premature, as
he did not surrender until October 18. The loss of his naval
protection, however, had made his position untenable.*

Sir I Received your favour and am Sorrow to hear of your illness We are all well through mercy There is now 14 Bushels of your Salt on hand It Sells Slow here oweing to the Scarcity of money It Sells on this Side only for 6 dollars a Bushel I had the news last night from fish kill that Admaral Rodney is defeated and came into New York with a few Shattered Ships and that Cornwalis was taken This is the general Report at the fish Kills In the utmost haste I Remain with my complyments to you and the Major and all

the familey   your freind and humble Servt.
                            Stephen Haight
Claverack Landing [Hudson]
September 26, 1781

37 *Philip Conine, Jr., of Coxsackie; Captain in the levies commanded by Lt. Col. Marinus Willett; to Leonard Bronk at Coxsackie.*

                            Patmiskasick 27th Sept. 1781
                            [South Cairo Great Plain]
Sir

The various Reports we have at this place of Lord Cornwallis being taken a prisoner, has induced me to send the Bearer down. I hope you will be kind Enough to Let me have the particulars if any have been Received your way We have peaceable times amongst us as yet Capt. Dubois set of [off] for Schoharrie on Tuesday. The party is not yet Returned who went with him as a guard so that we have no Late Account from there. Tommorrow is the time when they are to be in & if any there is any thing new that way I shall do myself the pleasure to let you know it

                            I am Sir your Sinceer .
                            friend
                            Ph. Conine

38 *Leonard Gansevoort, Jr., of Albany; to Leonard Bronk at Coxsackie. The action described in the third paragraph was probably the last military engagement of the war on New York soil. "Young Butler" was Captain Walter Butler, who with his father, Colonel John Butler, was one of the most hated and feared Tory leaders of the Mohawk Valley. His scalp was sold in Albany.*

                            4 Nov. 1781
My dear Sir

I most heartily congratulate you on the great and glorious News of the surrender of Cornwallis Yesterday we testified our Joy with the firing of Cannon, Ringing of Bells & drinking and eating plentifully Every thing was conducted with a regularity and order which does Honour to the

Citizens of this place [Albany] I hope your good Whigs at Cooksackie will also celebrate the Day Nothing will excuse you for not doing it Let every Heart be glad Let every Friend to his Country rejoice and let those dastardly Villians the Torys with dejected Spirit and drooping in Silence and Sorrow curse the Day that they became Enemies to their Country

My Friend I am overjoyed So are all good and true Whigs It gives me Pleasure to see the Mortification of those Miscreants whose Souls are as Black as Hell and whose Minds are as dark as the Midnight Shades I could write a whole Day but Mr. Gay waits impatiently for my Letter

A little more News and then I shall leave off Yesterday Letters arrived from Col. Willet who is arrived at Fort Renselier He says he pursued the Enemy until his provisions was quite exhausted He has however had an Engagement with the Rear Guard of the Enemy and has killed Nine of them & taken twenty Prisoners Among the killed is Young Butler They say the Oneyda Indians have scalped him This is certain that he is killed and that Part of his Cloaths and Ornaments have already been sold at Schenectady I think the Expedition has been a pretty dear One to the Enemy

Lord Stirling writes that the Enemy are not advancing further than Ticonderoga so that we need fear nothing from there

Once more I give you Joy so I do your Father and Mother and all who stand connected with you Rejoice with an exceeding great Joy If you dont the Tories will think you are still afraid

believe me your Friend
L G

39 *Benjamin Van Orden of the Great Imboght; to Leonard Bronk at Coxsackie.*

Catskill Landing
December 4th 1781

Sir

I received a Letter from Coll. [Colonel] Hay Last Night by which he Informs me of the Necessity the Army is in for want of flour and requests of me that I shall use my Best Endeavours to Obtain as much as Lays in my power You will therefore See the Necessity of Geting Ground what is in your mill if it is not Already Done, as I expect a Sloop to fetch it Away if the Season will permitt, but however it Does not ~~Look~~ Likely at present but it is always good to be ready if an opportunity Should offer Wrigh me a Line About the Wheat whether any is Brought in or not that the Law may be put in Execution against Delinquits,

De Grotenis aen Your Self Wife and fathers family from your Humble Servent

Benjamin Van Orden

40 *Leonard Gansevoort, Jr., of Albany; to Leonard Bronk at Coxsackie.*

Saturday Evening 8 OClock
December 1781

Dear Sir

Mr. Gay informs me that your little Boy is quite sick I am extreamly Sorry for it I could wish you was here where you might have an Opportunity of having the assistance of skilful Physicans who might possibly help him If his Situation is such as that it would admit of your coming up with him I would advise you to do it, our House is at your Service and our Aid in every Instance you may rest assured of

Every Person I see from your Quarter tells me something about my old Friend Arent What to think of it I know not I can hardly think he is gone to New York He is I am persuaded no *Tory* but where he can be gone is to a Mistery that I for my Part cannot see through His good Nature has undone him I therefore pity him Heaven knows what will become of his poor Family Distress and want will assuredly await them

Mr. Gay says you want to know upon what Footing the New Money stands I am sorry to tell you that it does not by any Means pass equal to Gold & Silver 40 for one it passes for Currently but no more The Legislature intend at their sitting here this Winter to raise the Value of it if possible and I hope they may effect it

Polly has been very unwell but is recovering fast My eldest Child has been unwell for two or three Days with a Cold

Polly joins with me in wishing your Parents yourself and wife the Compliments of the Season and a Continuance of Earthly Enjoyments

I am Sir
Your Friend sincerely
L. Gansevoort Junr.

41 *Henry Oothoudt of Albany to Leonard Bronk at Coxsackie. David Abeel mentioned below was taken prisoner during a Tory-Indian raid on his homestead. With others, he subsequently escaped from Canada.*

Albany 18th Dec. 1781

Dear Sir
Mr. David Abeel has been with me this Day and Informed me that last April when he was taken prisoner and Carried to Niagara amongst the rest of the party took from him Two Certificates given by you as Assistant Agent for the State for 50 Bushel of wheat That he has Applied to you to have the Certificates renewed and you had refered the matter to Collo. [Colonel] Hay and Collo. [Colonel] Hay had given as his Opinion that if Mr. Abeel gave you Security to Indemnify you against the said Certificates you might renew them Mr. Abeel tells me he Cannot pay his Tax without the said Certificates and offers that he will give Security to you for Indemnifying you against them that no person will Claim the same against the State For he must assign them and will give you Security to Indemnify you if the State will not Allow the Certificates you give This offer of Mr. Abeel I think a generous offer and you may give him the Certificates upon Collo. [Colonel] Hays Opinion who is your principal with whom you have to Settle with
My respect I am Sir
Your Humble Servt.
Heny. Oothoudt

42 *Leonard Gansevoort, Jr., of Albany; to Leonard Bronk at Coxsackie.*

Albany 30 June 1782

Dear Sir
I inclose you three Letters which I must beg you to forward
I expected to have seen you in Town on the Occasion of

Genl. Washington's arrival It was well worth your while to come thus far to see the greatest character in the world, who has no equal in History I am surprized that numbers have not come from the Country to see the Deliverer of their Country who has given them Independence and will ere long I am persuaded give them Peace Last Friday he left this Place and went to Saragtoga From there he went to Schenectady where he dined and last Evening again arrived here

We have no News in this Quarter at all I am informed that the Levies are all ordered down If this is so and I believe it is true we will again lay exposed to the inroads of the Enemy

I think I wrote you some Time ago about a Barrel of mine at Hans Spoors Is it at your House? If it is not I could wish you would request Spoor to bring it to your House or else to pay for it a Dollar If he will do neither I wish you would speak to your Father to commence a Suit against him in my Name for the value of the Barrel This I do because the Man has acted the mean and unmanly Part You can want no Proff of his having the Barrel He will not deny it

I wish you and yours all well Tell your wife she must come and see our 3d Daughter and if she likes it can take it with her as a Pattern to copy after Tell her also that if she does not come up we will be down after Harvest

Give Polly's and my best Respects to your Parents I wish you Health and Happiness and an Heir

Your's
L G Junr.

43 *Leonard Bronk of Coxsackie, assistant state agent; expenses incurred in the years 1780 and 1781 for the movement of military supplies of cattle, wheat and other grains from the Great Imboght and the Coxsackie Districts to Albany.*

An Account of the Contingent Expences from Leonard Bronk Assist State Agent in behalf of Collo. [Colonel] Udny Hay Agent for the State of New York

	Whom Servises Performed	Amount of Pay		
1780		£	S	d
August 7	Benjemin Tryon Three days in Servise for gethering Cattle			

Date	Description			
	and Driving them from Coxseghkie to Albany at Two Dollars of New-Emision per Day	2	8	—
Do	Thomas Gay Two Days Do	1	12	—
Do	Peter Tryon Three Do Do	2	8	—
Do	John L Bronk for keeping 3 hd of Cattle one Day & Night	—	3	—
Do	Theunes Van Veghten for Delivering his Beast at Coxh. [Coxsackie]	—	8	—
Sept 15th	Thoms. Gay Three Days with Two hands for Gethering Cattle at Coxseghkie & Driving them to Albany at Two Dolls. pr hand	4	16	—
Do	William V. D. Berck Do Two Days	1	12	—
Do	Richard H. V. D. Berck Do Do	1	12	—
Do	Robt. V. D. Berck for keepg. 5 hd. of Cattle one Night in pasture	—	5	—
Do	Thomas Gay Five Days for Gethering Cattle at Great Imbought & Driving them to Albany at Two Dolls pr Day	4	—	—
Do	Ricd. Van D. Berck Four Days Do	3	4	—
Do	Robt, V. D. Berck for keeping 9 head of Cattle one Night in pasture	—	8	—
Octr 9th	To Hendk Van Wie for Taking up one Creature Strayed from the Drivers & Keeping the same Twenty Days in pasture	1	4	—
Octr 12th	Gosa Heremanse for Transport. from Store to the Landg.	—		
1781				
Jany, 19th	Thoms. Gay Two Days for Driving Cattle from this place to Albany at 2 Dolls. pr.			

	Day	1	12	—
Do	Richd. H. V. D. Berck Do	1	12	—
Do	William Van Den Berck Do	1	12	—
Do	Phillip Conine Thomas Gay & Richard Bronk for Appg. 11 hd. of Cattle	2	8	—
Do	Cornelius Dubois for Storage &	4	8	—
Dec 31	Michl. Colyer for Driving Cattle 2 Days at 2 Dolls. pr. day	1	12	—
Jany. 31st	Phillip Conine & Ricd. Bronk for Appraifg. Seven hd. Cattle	—	16	—
Feby. 2nd	Jonas Bronk & Peter Conine for Driving Cattle from Coxseghkie to Albany Each Five Days to Two Dolls. pr.	3	4	—
Do	Phillip Conine Richard Bronk & Thomas Gay for appraising Seven head of Cattle Each at 6 pr. head	1	4	—
Jany. 16th.	Teunis Van Vechten transported Two Leads of Flour from Catskill to Albany	5	4	—
Do	John L Bronk Twenty Bushs. of Barley & four Do. Oats Transported to Albany from Coxseghkie	2	—	—
Do	Richard Van Den Berck for Transporting 14 Bushs. Oats four Do. Rye & Five Do. Indian Corn from Do. to Do.	2	—	—
Do 26th	John L Bronk for Transporting 20 Bushs. of Wheat from Coxseghkie Landg. to Patroons Mills Albany	2	—	—
Do	Phillip Bronk Do	2	—	—
Do	Anthony Van Bergen Do	2	—	—
Do	William Van D. Berck Do	2	—	—
Do 22nd	Abm. Halenbeck 15 Bush. of Oats Do	—	18	—
Do 29th	William Groom Do 23 3/4 Oats from Lonenburgh to Do	2	—	—

Do 30th	Peter Van Slyck 20 Bushs. of Wheat	2	—	—
Do 31st	Petrus Overpagh 8 Do Wh: 7½ Rye & 4 Do I. Corn from Catskill to Albany	2	8	—
Feby 1st	Willm. Brandw. Transporg. Fifteen Bushs. Wh. & Ten Bushs. Oats from Loneng. to Albany	2	8	—
Do 6th	Saml. Van Veghten one Load of Flour From Catskill to Albany	2	8	—
Do 8	Dirick Spoor Transporting 23 Bushs. of Wheat from Coxs. Distt. to Albany Pats. Mills 28 Miles	2	8	—
Do 15	Willm. & Lawe. Salisby. for Delivering Cattle out G. Imt. Distt. to Alby. Each 3 Days at 2 Dolls. pr. Day	4	16	—
Do	Joeham. [?] Colyer Do Do	2	8	—
March 1st	John L Bronk Two Loads of flour	4	—	—
	Robt. V. D. Berck Do	4	—	—
10th	Thoms. Gay one Do	2	—	—
	Do Forage Transport	0	16	—

44 *Leonard Gansevoort, Jr., of Albany; to Leonard Bronk at Coxsackie.*

25th Oct. 1782

Dear Leonard

Hard Times I have no Butter and am now obliged to send my Negro down to you for some He has Money to pay for whatever he can get Assist him if you please and oblige your Friend

Polly says she wants some Vineger If you can help her to some you will do her a kindness We want a great many Things for the Winter and I find a great Scarcity of those Things which are most necessary

Hoe gaet is het haesh Bonne I long to drink the Wine which you will owe me if a Daughter should make her appearance and gladden your Ears with that agreeable Sound called Matrimonial Music   I have enough of it

Good News   They really say it is a Fact that the Enemy purpose to quit New York   Then I am sure we will have Reason to rejoice with an exceeding great Joy

and cry out with a loud voice

Huzza for the Congress and General Washington

I must go to Court to try a Cause   Therefore I must leave off the not without my Compliments to your Rib and Respects to the old People

Kiss your Wife for me and tell her at the same time I had rather do it myself

Thine Sincerely

L G. Junr.

45 *Leonard Gansevoort, Jr., of Albany; to Leonard Bronk at Coxsackie.*

Albany 12th Feby. 1783

Dr. Sir

The Bearer of this Letter will deliver you a Frock for your little one   I wish she may live to wear it out entirely

You told me that Boskerk would bring me Hay   He has not yet done it   I wish you would take the Trouble to let him know that I expect him and if he does not bring it, I shall most assuredly bear hard upon him, as I do not intend to be trifled with any longer.

Polly begins to grow uneasy whenever she looks at her little Store of Butter   If you can help her without putting yourself to Inconvenience (which I would not by any means you should do) you will greatly oblidge her

I suppose you have heard before now of the Western Expedition   I for my Part do not like it as I am afraid it will irritate the Indians and bring them again upon our Backs next Summer   However small Folks like you and me must acquiesce and say amen

I wish you and your wife Health   We are well   God bless you

Your Friend

L. G. Junr.

dont read this Letter till you have read the other

46 *Leonard Gansevoort, Jr., of Albany; to Leonard Bronk at Coxsackie.*

Albany 13th March 1783

Dr. Sir

Mr. Gay the Bearer of this Letter will Deliver you a Frock for your little Miss and the Tea Spoons which I have had made for you They are made according to the present fashion I hope they please you As for the Table Spoons they are not yet finished The Reason is because Mr. Lansing has not yet the Silver to make them of nor have I been able to get it for him, tho I have endeavored by every means in my power He wants fifteen dollars to make them up If you have as much with you and will send it up I will get him to make them immediately

The enclosed Letter I send you that you may see that I have thought of you, the Person who was to take it did not call for it

We have been in a perfect State of Peace here for some Time past of late There has again been heard a Cry of War, but it proceeds from a Few Merchants who would not care if all the Inhabitants of America went to Perdition provided they could remain secure and enrich themselves Many of them I hope will suffer In fact they will deserve it as they have been sucking the Blood of their Fellow Citizens and have as Scripture so prefers it grinded the Face of the Poor. It is the general opinion of those who can and who have a Right to think that it will be Peace Every Manevure of the Enemy at New York plainly indicates Even should the War continue the Governor and Genl. Washington are both of Opinion that they will quit the Continent which if they do will be better for us than a State of Perfect Peace

Our Friend the Fat Recorder is of opinion that he will loose [lose] Money by his Contract It does not seem however to give him much uneasiness He eats drinks sleeps and sings as he always did He is a happy Mortal

I long to see you I have plenty of Hay and Grain for your Horse and a good warm
Bed for yourself if you will come and see me

I am somewhat hurried with Business or I would write more My Love to Mrs. Bronck Kiss her for Me as also your little one Polly joins me in wishing you and Tyny Health

God bless you
Yours
L. G. Junr.

BN. Mr. Gay very fortunately brought us some Butter or we would have been out

47 *John Wigram of Manor Livingston [Columbia County]; to Leonard Bronk at Coxsackie.*

Manor Livingston March 27 1783
My Dear Friend
Permit me to congratulate you on the Treaty of Peace being signed by all the Powers at War which was to take place the 21 Inst in America Col. Harry Livingston recd. a Letter from the Governor by Express Last Evening informing of his having Reced. the News by Express from Col. Floyd one of our Delegates in Congress that the Packett was arrived in Delaware a few Miles below Philadelphia but her Dispatches was not landed. His Letter was dated the 21st Inst. The Governor desires Col. Harry to spread this News to all the good Citizens but that no Public demonstration of Joy may be testified till he has Officially sent orders
I am my Dear Friend
Yours Sincerely
John Wigram

48 *Leonard Gansevoort, Jr., of Albany; to Leonard Bronk at Coxsackie.*

Albany 17th June 1783
Sir
I received your last Letter I am glad to hear that you have Flouer [flour] to spare as I am entirely out I shall send Harry down this Week for it The Money I will pay shortly as I expect to receive a large sum from a Man who has been indebted to me for a long Time, and I shall then pay off the Remainder of what I owe the old Gentleman
I have sent you by Mr. Gay some Wafers and Sealing Wax which I have taken of my own Stock as there are none to be had in Town I must beg your acceptance of them
In about three Weeks I do intend to go Down to New York I wish you could get ready to go also at that Time as I should

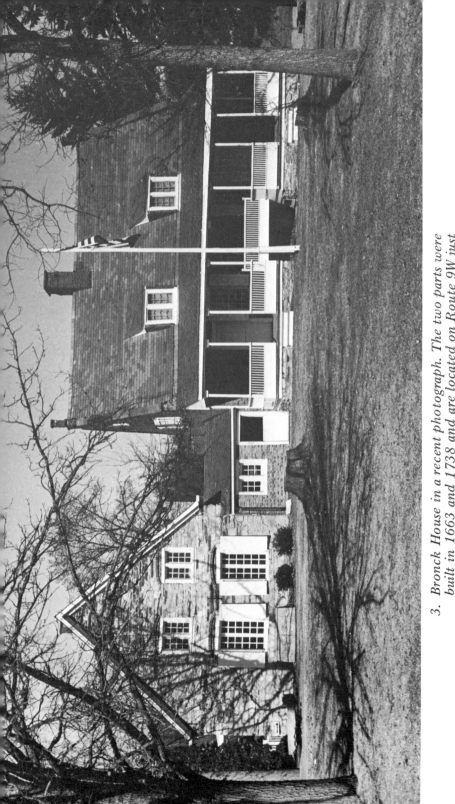

3. *Bronck House in a recent photograph. The two parts were built in 1663 and 1738 and are located on Route 9W just east of the village of Coxsackie, New York.*

like your Company Try whether you can't get ready to
go I go in the Recorder's Sloop who goes down himself

Tuesday next the 25th of this Month is St. John's Day
when we are to walk in Procession We have all the Musick of
the New York Line, which will be a great Addition to it I
dare say it will be the most elegant Procession that ever was
in this Place You must come up to see us walk tho you do
not join in it I would advise you to come next Monday as
the Procession will be about ten O'Clock in the Morning As
you never have seen a Thing of this kind I give my Honour it
is worth seeing The Musick will make it beyond Description
entertaining You must bring Tyny with you to see it I am
certain it will give her Pleasure

Polly says she is determined not to come down to
Cooksakie again till you and your Wife have been here You
cannot but admit she is right We will do every Thing in our
Power to make you both happy if you do come

We live peaceable and happy Every Thing is coming again
into its old Channel The Sloops come loaded from New
York with every good and valuable article The Prices of all
Kinds of goods are low

I wish you and your Wife Health Kiss the little girl for me

Remember me to the Old People I expect to find your
Father grown at least ten years younger by the Peace and
your Mother about fifteen. God bless you all

Your Friend

Leon. Gansevoort, Junr.

Bibliography

Beauchamp, William M., *Aboriginal Place Names of New York*. Albany: New York State Education Department, 1907.

Beers, J. B., *History of Greene County*, New York. New York: J. B. Beers & Company, 1884.

Braeman, John, *The Road to Independence; A Documentary History of the Causes of the American Revolution: 1763–1776*. New York: G. P. Putman's Sons, 1963.

Greene County Historical Society, *The "Old Times" Corner, First Series*; edited by George Halcott Chadwick and Jessie Van Vechten Vedder. Catskill, N. Y., 1932.

Halsey, Francis Whiting, *The Old New York Frontier.* Mineola, N.Y.: Ira J. Friedman Inc. Reprint.

Kenney, Alice P., *The Gansevoorts of Albany*. Syracuse, N. Y.: Syracuse University Press, 1969.

Ketchum, Richard M., Ed., *The American Heritage Book of the Revolution*. New York: American Heritage Publishing Company, 1958.

Lossing, Benson J., *The Pictorial Field Book of The Revolution*. 2 vols., New York: Harper & Brothers, 1855.

New York (State), *The American Revolution in New York; Its Political Social and Economic Significance*. Albany, N.Y.: The University of the State of New York, Division of Archives and History, 1926.

New York (State), *Minutes of the Albany Committee of Correspondence 1775–1778,* Vol. 1. Albany: The University of the State of New York, The Division of Archives and History, 1923.

New York (State), *New York in the American Revolution as Colony and State.* Albany, 1898.

New York (State), *New York in the Revolution as Colony and State; Supplement.* Albany, N. Y., 1901.

New York (State), *Orderly Books of the Fourth New York Regiment, 1778–1780. The Second New York Regiment, 1780-1783.* Albany: The University of the State of New York, Division of Archives and History, 1932.

New York State Historical Association, *History of the State of New York,* ed. by Alexander C. Flick. New York: Columbia University Press, 1933. Volume 111: *Whig and Tory.*

Reid, W. Max, *The Mohawk Valley; Its Legends and Its History.* New York: G. P. Putman's Sons, 1904.

Stone, William L., *Life of Joseph Brant—Thayendanegea, Including the Indian Wars of the American Revolution.* Vol. 1. New York: George Dearborn & Co., 1838.

Van Schaack, H. C., Ed., *The Life of Peter Van Schaack.* New York, 1842.

Vedder, Jessie Van Vechten, *History of Greene County, 1651–1800.* Catskill, N. Y., 1927.

Index of Names

References are to numbered documents. In parentheses following certain names will be found either the earlier surname spelling or a variety of known spellings. Where uncertainties continued to exist, even after extensive research, the names are listed as written in the documents.